# Introduction

In this, my first book, I have shared a variety of designs—something for every quilter.

A fascination with the Double Arrow block started when a friend shared a photo of the block from the June 1933 issue of *The Kansas City Star*. For easy and traditional piecing, try my version of this block in Double Arrow, or check out Autumn Leaves.

If you want to add a little appliqué to your traditional quilt, you might like Fly Away Home.

If you lean toward modern styles, take a look at Dream Weaver. It's a row quilt with some fun dimensional flowers.

Try Lily & Friends if you really enjoy dimensional flowers. This quilt is sure to delight, as the flowers literally pop off the quilt. Many years ago I heard someone say they had seen a quilt where the flowers stood an inch off the quilt. Since then I have made many quilts with stuffed appliqué.

How about making the formal-looking runner Black Tie Event—it makes a nice shower gift for a bride-to-be. Make the double heart and doves in her wedding colors. The double open heart is inspired by a jewelry design.

How about adding some wool appliqué to your batik project? The project Friends does just that. Small scraps of wool make the little people that are placed in a circle around the center. Hang the quilt on a wall or display it on a table. Make one for you and one for a friend.

Want a larger take-along project? Wildflowers might be the quilt for you. The cover quilt incorporates embroidered vines with lots of small wool appliquéd flowers on a pieced background.

If you are like me, you like to turn quilts over to look at the quilting. Sometimes there is a nice surprise. One of the things I like to do is make one extra block, or one extra piece of appliqué. This serves two purposes—it lets me select the best for the front of the quilt, and it gives me something to make into a label to add to the back.

I hope you will find lots of inspiration in these projects. I have very much enjoyed designing and sewing these projects for you.

—Bev Getschel

# Meet the Designer

Bev Getschel's story starts the same as many; she cannot remember a time when she wasn't sewing. Her mother sewed and started her on primitive doll clothes as soon as she could hold a needle and thread. In high school she made garments for herself, her sister and her friends. Then she continued by making clothes for her children, finally graduating to evening gowns and costumes.

In 2003, she stumbled onto quilting, and it was a great fit. Retiring from hairdressing in 2004 gave her time to pursue her newfound hobby.

At first, she pursued competition quilts with some success on a regional level, but she soon discovered it was the design process she enjoyed most. Bev has had well over 100 featured patterns published in major quilt magazines.

Bev's unique style of blending traditional patterns with her own flavor of appliqué to create upscale eclectic finishes will amaze and delight all quilters. Her patterns are clear, stylish and appeal to all skill levels.

# Table of Contents

Autumn Leaves,
*page 40*

Black Tie,
*page 8*

# Friends

This fun wall hanging could easily be personalized by adding names or dates to it. The possibilities are endless if you use your imagination.

## Specifications

Skill Level: Confident Beginner
Quilt Size: 31" x 31"
Block Size: 8" x 8" finished
Number of Blocks: 1

## Materials

- Scraps medium and dark felted wool
- 1 fat eighth medium brown batik
- ¾ yard multicolored batik
- 1¼ yards cream batik
- Backing to size
- Batting to size
- Thread
- Black pearl cotton
- ½ yard 18"-wide lightweight fusible web
- Basic sewing tools and supplies

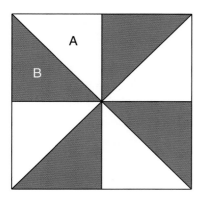

**Pinwheel**
8" x 8" Finished Block
Make 1

## Cutting

### From scraps felted wool:

- Prepare pieces for fusible appliqué as per patterns using templates given on insert and instructions.

### From medium brown batik:

- Cut 1 (4⅞" x 21") strip.
  Subcut strip into 2 (4⅞") squares. Cut each square in half on 1 diagonal to make 4 B triangles.

### From multicolored batik:

- Cut 1 (6½" by fabric width) strip.
  Subcut strip into 12 (3½" x 6½") E rectangles.
- Cut 1 (5½" by fabric width) strip.
  Subcut strip into 1 (5½" x 12½") bow strip and 1 (4" x 4½") knot strip.
- Cut 4 (2¼" by fabric width) binding strips.

### From cream batik:

- Cut 2 (7" by fabric width) strips.
  Subcut strips into 2 (7" x 21½") D rectangles, 2 (7" x 8½") C rectangles and 2 (4⅞") squares. Cut the squares in half on 1 diagonal to make 4 A triangles.
- Cut 3 (2" by fabric width) strips.
  Subcut strips into 48 (2") F squares.
- Cut 1 (3½" by fabric width) strip.
  Subcut strip into 8 (2" x 3½") G rectangles and 4 (3½") H squares.
- Cut 4 (2½" by fabric width) strips.
  Trim strips to make 2 each 2½" x 27½" I strips and 2½" x 31½" J strips.

## Completing the Pinwheel Block

**1.** Sew A to B along the diagonal to make an A-B unit as shown in Figure 1; press. Repeat to make a total of four A-B units.

A-B Unit
Make 4

Make 2

**Figure 1**          **Figure 2**

**2.** Join two A-B units to make a row as shown in Figure 2; press. Repeat to make a second row.

**3.** Join the rows referring to Figure 3 to complete the Pinwheel block; press.

**Figure 3**

## Completing the Pieced Background

**1.** Referring to Figure 4, sew a C rectangle to opposite sides of the Pinwheel block; press. Add D rectangles to opposite long sides of the pieced block unit to complete the pieced center; press.

**Figure 4**

**2.** Mark a diagonal line from corner to corner on the wrong side of each F square.

**3.** Referring to Figure 5, place an F square on one corner of an E rectangle and stitch on the marked line; trim seam allowance to ¼" and press F open.

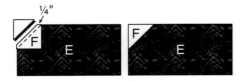

**Figure 5**

**4.** Repeat step 3 on each corner of E to complete an E-F unit as shown in Figure 6.

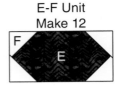
E-F Unit
Make 12

**Figure 6**

**5.** Repeat steps 3 and 4 to complete a total of 12 E-F units.

**6.** Join three E-F units with two G rectangles to make a side strip as shown in Figure 7; press. Repeat to make a total of four side strips.

Make 4

**Figure 7**

**7.** Sew a side strip to opposite sides of the pieced center; press.

**8.** Sew an H square to each end of each remaining side strip; press. Sew these strips to the remaining sides of the pieced center; press.

**9.** Sew I strips to opposite sides and J strips to the top and bottom of the pieced center; press.

**10.** Measure 5½" from the corner along each side and mark as shown in Figure 8.

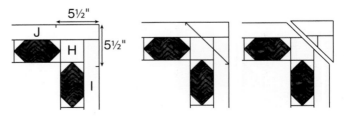

**Figure 8**          **Figure 9**

**11.** Draw a line to connect the marks at each corner and trim to make angled corners to complete the pieced background as shown in Figure 9.

## Completing the Appliqué

**1.** Trace head, shirt and pants shapes onto the paper side of the fusible web 12 times. Cut out shapes leaving a margin around each one.

**2.** Fuse shapes to the wool using a pressing cloth or parchment paper to protect the wool, if necessary.

**3.** Cut out shapes on traced lines; remove paper backing.

**4.** Using a water-erasable marker, draw a circle around the center block starting the circle about ¼" from the outer corners of the Pinwheel block as shown in Figure 10.

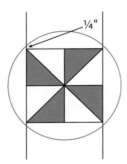

**Figure 10**

**5.** Starting at those corners, place one motif (head, shirt and pants) at each corner, overlapping shirt on top of the pants, and pin in place. Arrange and pin two motifs between each of the pinned motifs, rearranging as necessary to make an even circle of motifs around the center block. Arms are extra long and may be trimmed as necessary where one arm touches another as shown in Figure 11.

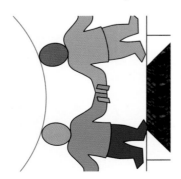

**Figure 11**

**6.** When satisfied with positioning, fuse in place to hold temporarily; remove pins. Lay pressing cloth or parchment paper on top of the motifs and hold iron in place for 4–6 seconds to secure. Turn the fused top wrong side up and iron over the fused shapes from the wrong side.

**7.** Using black pearl cotton and a blanket stitch, hand-stitch around each shape to secure.

**8.** Referring to shirt pattern, use black pearl cotton and a running stitch to stitch the heart shapes and connecting lines from motif to motif.

## Completing the Quilt

**1.** Create a quilt sandwich referring to Finishing Your Quilt on page 48.

**2.** Quilt as desired.

**3.** Bind referring to Finishing Your Quilt on page 48.

**4.** Fold the bow strip in half with right sides together along length; stitch along the long open edge to make a tube. Turn right side out and press with seam centered as shown in Figure 12.

**Figure 12**

### Here's a Tip

*Cut a rectangle and add a narrow border all around to end up with a block that is at least 9½" x 7". Cut two extra appliqué motifs and appliqué to the block. Then stitch block to the bottom of the back side of the quilt to make a label. Personalize with the recipient's name or a message to make a special gift.*

**5.** Referring to Figure 13, fold strip into a bow shape and pin ends at the center back to hold. Baste through the center to hold ends in place.

**Figure 13**

**6.** Repeat step 4 with the knot strip. Wrap the stitched knot strip around the folded bow strip and hand-stitch ends together to secure.

**7.** Position and hand-stitch the bow in the lower right-hand corner, referring to the Placement Diagram for positioning.

**8.** Prepare and attach a hanging sleeve on the top back side to complete the quilt referring to Making a Hanging Sleeve sidebar at right. ●

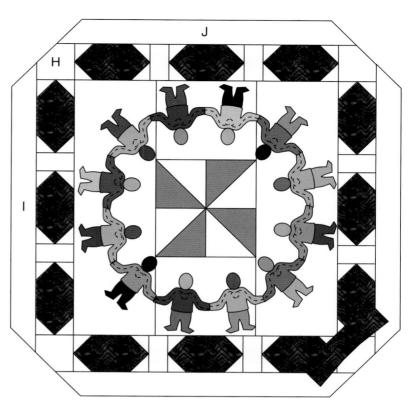

**Friends**
Placement Diagram 31" x 31"

# Making a Hanging Sleeve

*Wall quilts may be hung using bone rings, tabs or using a hanging sleeve to fit on a rod.*

*The size of the hanging sleeve depends on the diameter of the rod. Smaller wall quilts use a narrower rod while larger quilts require something more sturdy.*

*To make a hanging sleeve to fit a quilt, cut a strip of fabric (or strips to join) 6"–10" wide and at least 1½" longer than the width of the edge of the quilt.*

*Turn under each end of strip ¼" and press. Turn under ½" again and press; stitch to hem.*

*Fold the hemmed strip with right sides together along the length and stitch. Press seam open. Turn right side out and press with seam centered.*

*Center the sleeve on the top back side of the quilt and hand-stitch the top edge in place.*

*Hand-stitch the back side of the sleeve to the quilt backing ½" from the bottom pressed edge. This allows space for the rod while preventing pulling on the front of the quilt (Figure A).*

*Stitch the hemmed edges touching the quilt back in place to finish (Figure B).*

*Some quilters like to insert the hanging sleeve into the seam at the top edge when sewing binding to the quilt edge.*

*To hang the quilt, insert the dowel or rod through the sleeve.*

½"

**Figure A**

seam line

**Figure B**

# Black Tie Event

Create a formal mood when you add this runner to your table.

## Specifications

Skill Level: Confident Beginner
Runner Size: 36" x 24"
Block Size: 8½" x 8½" finished
Number of Blocks: 4

## Materials

- 1 fat eighth light gray solid
- 1 fat quarter orange tonal
- 1 fat quarter each 4 different black tonals
- 1 fat quarter each 4 different white tonals
- ⅓ yard black tonal
- Backing to size
- Batting to size
- Thread
- 10" or larger square ruler
- 2 black seed beads
- Masking tape
- Basic sewing tools and supplies

## Cutting

Prepare templates for swirl and bird pieces using templates given on insert. Cut as per patterns and instructions.

## From light gray solid:

- Cut bird motif pieces as per pattern and instructions.

## From orange tonal:

- Cut swirls as per pattern and instructions.

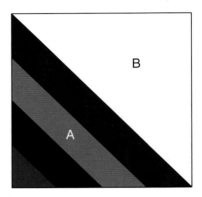

**Black Tie Event**
8½" x 8½" Finished Block
Make 4

## From black tonal fat quarters:

- Cut a total of 28 (2" x 21") A strips.

## From white tonal fat quarters:

- Cut 2 (9⅜") squares.
    Cut each square in half on 1 diagonal to make
       4 B triangles.
- Cut 3 (9") C squares.

## From black tonal yardage:

- Cut 3 (2¼" by fabric width) binding strips.

## Completing the Blocks

**1.** Select and join four A strips with right sides together along length to make an A strip set; press. Repeat to make a total of seven A strip sets.

**2.** Place a piece of masking tape from the 9⅜" line on one side to the 9⅜" line on the adjacent side of the square ruler to mark a 9⅜" triangle.

**3.** Place the marked ruler on an A strip set and cut one A triangle as shown in Figure 1; place marked ruler on opposite edge of A strip set as shown in Figure 2 and repeat to cut a total of two A triangles from the strip set. Repeat to cut a total of 14 A triangles.

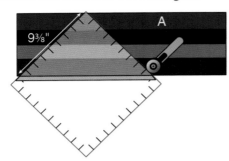

**Figure 1**

**Figure 2**

**4.** Sew an A triangle to a B triangle to complete one Black Tie block as shown in Figure 3; press. Repeat to make a total of four blocks.

**Figure 3**

**Black Tie Event**
Placement Diagram 36" x 24"

## Completing the Runner

Refer to the Placement Diagram for positioning of pieces.

**1.** Arrange and join the Black Tie blocks with the C squares and remaining A triangles in diagonal rows as shown in Figure 4 to complete the runner top; press.

**Figure 4**

**2.** Prepare bird and swirl pieces for hand appliqué referring to Needle-Turn Applique on pages 32 and 33.

**3.** Arrange and pin the swirl pieces on the runner top, overlapping heart-shape ends in the center. Turning under the seam allowance as you stitch, hand-stitch the swirl shapes in place.

**4.** Arrange and pin a bird motif in place on the heart end of the swirls. Appliqué in place as in step 3.

**5.** Create a quilt sandwich referring to Finishing Your Quilt on page 48.

**6.** Quilt as desired.

**7.** Bind referring to Finishing Your Quilt on page 48.

**8.** Hand-stitch a black seed bead on each bird for eye to finish. ●

# Lily & Friends

Bring your flower garden inside and enjoy the blooms all year-round. Add stuffed 3-D appliqué flowers and a bit of stitching to make this fun and easy project.

## Specifications

Skill Level: Intermediate
Quilt Size: 24" x 36"
Block Size: 6" x 6" finished
Number of Blocks: 12

## Materials

- Assorted bright-color (including medium and dark purple, yellow and green) batik scraps
- 1 fat eighth white solid
- ¾ yard light green batik
- 1 yard cream batik
- Backing to size
- Batting to size
- Thread
- 6-strand embroidery floss to match assorted bright-color batik scraps
- Polyester fiberfill or batting scraps
- Basic sewing tools and supplies

## Cutting

### From assorted bright-color batik scraps:

- Cut flower and leaf shapes using templates given on insert and referring to 3-D Appliqué on pages 14 and 15.

### From white solid:

- Cut small flowers using templates given on insert and referring to 3-D Appliqué on pages 14 and 15.

### From light green batik:

- Cut 2 (2½" by fabric width) B strips.
- Cut 1 (6½" by fabric width) strip.
  Subcut strip into 16 (2½" x 6½") C rectangles.
- Cut 4 (2¼" by fabric width) binding strips.

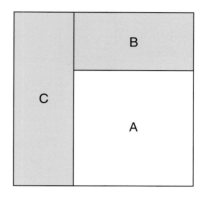

**Faux Attic Window**
6" x 6" Finished Block
Make 12

### From cream batik:

- Cut 2 (4½" by fabric width) A strips.
- Cut 4 (2½" by fabric width) strips.
  Trim strips to make 2 each 2½" x 24½" F and 2½" x 32½" E strips.
- Cut 1 (8½" by fabric width) strip.
  Subcut strip into 1 (8½" x 20½") D strip.

## Completing the Blocks

**1.** Sew an A strip to a B strip with right sides together along length to make an A-B strip set; press. Repeat to make a second strip set.

**2.** Subcut the A-B strip sets into 12 (4½" x 6½") A-B units as shown in Figure 1.

**3.** Sew a C strip to each A-B unit to complete a total of 12 Faux Attic Window blocks referring to the block drawing.

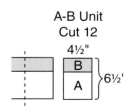

A-B Unit
Cut 12
4½"

**Figure 1**

## Completing the Quilt

**1.** Arrange and join the blocks with the extra C rectangles around the center D rectangle to complete the center background as shown in Figure 2; press.

**2.** Sew E strips to opposite long sides and F strips to the top and bottom of the center background; press.

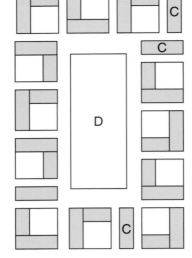

**Figure 2**

**3.** Using a water-erasable marker or pencil, mark curving lines on the center background using the curved vine stitching pattern given on insert and referring to Figure 3 for positioning, or draw the lines freehand as desired.

**4.** Create a quilt sandwich referring to Finishing Your Quilt on page 48.

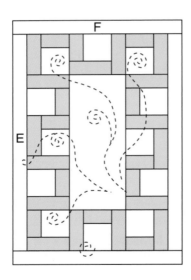

**Figure 3**

**5.** Quilt, echoing around the marked vine lines.

**6.** Add hanging sleeve, if desired. **Note:** See Making a Hanging Sleeve on page 7 for instructions.

**7.** Bind referring to Finishing Your Quilt on page 48.

## Here's a Tip

*Quilt the background before adding any of the appliqué or embroidery.*

**8.** Lay 6-strand lengths of green embroidery floss along the marked curving lines and couch-stitch in place using stitches about ¼" apart and matching green thread, referring to Figure 4.

**Figure 4**

**9.** Prepare and add the 3-D flowers and leaves referring to 3-D Appliqué on pages 14 and 15 to finish. ●

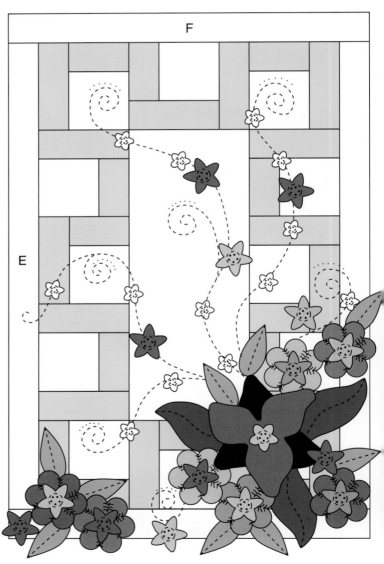

**Lily & Friends**
Placement Diagram 24" x 36"

# 3-D Appliqué

**1.** Trace flower and leaf templates on the wrong side of two layers of matching fabric for sets; pin centers and stitch on the traced lines as shown in Figure A.

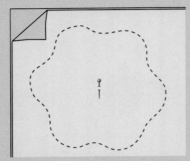

**Figure A**

**2.** Cut out stitched shapes ³⁄₁₆" from stitching lines and cut a slit in the back side only referring to Figure B.

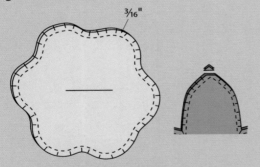

**Figure B**

**3.** Clip curves and corners, again referring to Figure B; turn right side out through the slits. Press edges flat.

**4.** Insert small batting scraps or polyester fiberfill in the petals of flowers and in leaf shapes to add dimension.

**5.** Hand-stitch a circle in the center of each star flower and pull thread to gather as shown in Figure C.

**Figure C**

**6.** Transfer lines from pattern to the small flowers. Hand-stitch on lines and pull to gather to complete.

**7.** Machine-stitch vein lines on leaves using matching thread referring to Figure D.

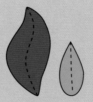

**Figure D**

**8.** Stitch lines between petals on the large flowers and pull to gather slightly as shown in Figure E.

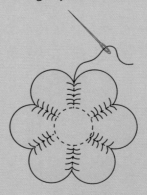

**Figure E**

**9.** Select a star flower and hand-stitch it inside one large flower, leaving petals loose as shown in Figure F. Repeat with remaining large flowers.

**Figure F**

**10.** Layer the two trillium flowers and add the small yellow flower in the center securing with five French knots made with 3 strands purple floss as shown in Figure G.

**Figure G**

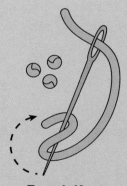

**French Knot**

**11.** Arrange and pin the completed trillium from step 10 on the right bottom corner of the quilted background, leaving room to cluster other flowers and leaves around it, referring to the Placement Diagram.

**12.** Add remaining flowers and leaves as desired and pin in place.

**13.** Stitch pieces in place with matching thread, folding up flower edges to attach beneath, leaving edges free referring to Figure H.

**Figure H**

**14.** Using 3 strands of embroidery floss, add seven French knots in the center of each star flower as shown in Figure I.

**Figure I**

**15.** Use 3 strands green floss to add seven French knots to upper edges of the couched curving lines referring to the curved vine stitching pattern given to finish.

# Dream Weaver

A fun and cheerful row quilt takes you from classic
to edgy with its quick and easy construction.

## Specifications

Skill Level: Confident Beginner
Quilt Size: 66" x 78"

## Materials

- 1 fat quarter white print
- 15 fat quarters assorted coordinating blue and purple prints
- ½ yard black solid or 13 yards premade ⅜" bias tape
- 3¼ yards white solid
- Backing to size
- Batting to size
- Thread
- ½ yard 18"-wide fusible web
- ⅜" bias maker
- 10 (⅝") yellow buttons
- Water-erasable marker or pencil
- Template material
- Basic sewing tools and supplies

## Cutting

### From white print:

- Cut 10 flower centers using templates given on insert as per instructions.

### From blue & purple prints:

- Select 1 fat quarter for flowers and cut shapes using templates given on insert as per instructions.
- Cut a total of 29 (4½" x 21") B strips.
- Cut a total of 17 (2¼" x 21") binding strips.

### From black solid:

- Cut ¾"-wide bias strips to total 450" when joined end to end.

### From white solid:

- Cut 15 (2½" by fabric width) strips.
  Subcut strips into 29 (2½" x 21") A strips.
- Cut 6 (6½" x 66½") C strips along remaining length of fabric.

## Completing the Quilt

**1.** Sew an A strip to a B strip with right sides together along length to make an A-B strip set; press. Repeat to make a total of 29 A-B strip sets.

**2.** Subcut the A-B strip sets into 231 (2½" x 6½") A-B units referring to Figure 1.

A-B Unit
Cut 231

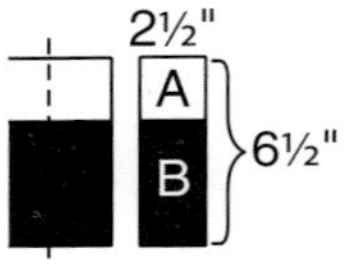

**Figure 1**

**3.** Select 33 A-B units and arrange and join the units to make an A-B row, turning every other unit when joining referring to Figure 2; press. Repeat to make a total of seven A-B rows.

A-B Row
Make 7

**Figure 2**

**4.** Prepare the bias strips for appliqué using the ⅜" bias maker and referring to manufacturer's instructions. Cut into six 75" lengths.

**5.** Prepare a template for the stem placement guide. Using the template as a guide, mark a curving line on each C strip with a water-erasable marker or pencil.

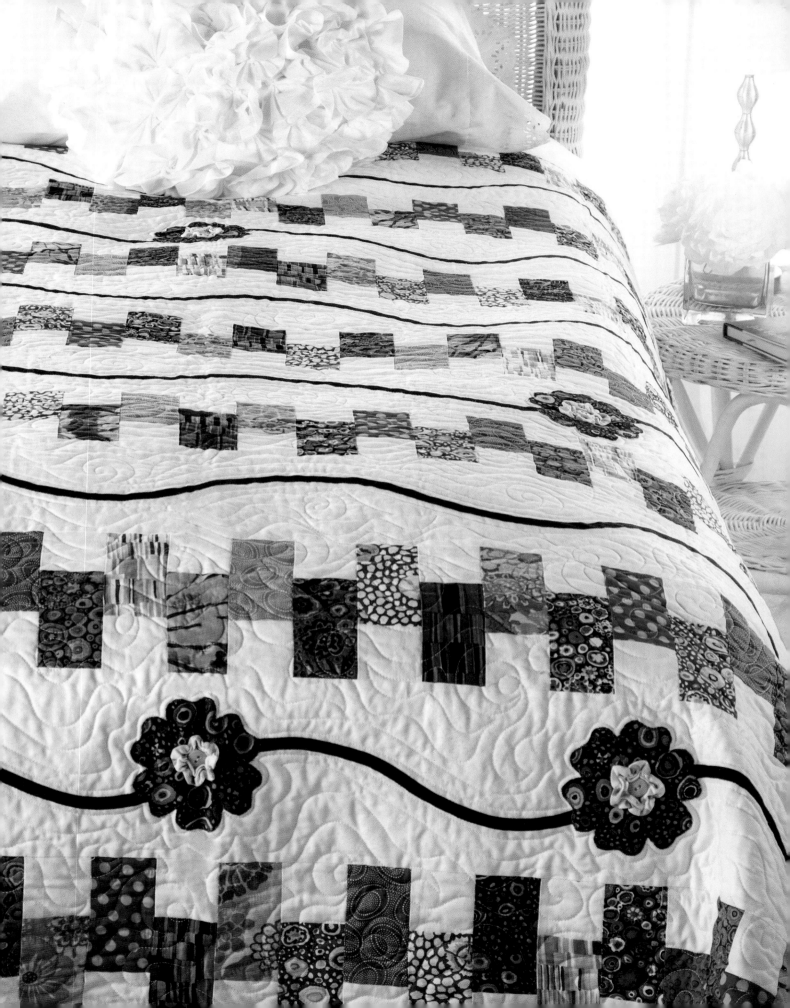

**6.** Center one 75" length of prepared bias on the marked line on one C strip, pinning at each end. Arrange in an undulating pattern across the strip referring to the Assembly Diagram for positioning. Machine-stitch in place with thread to match and a narrow zigzag stitch referring to Figure 3. Trim bias ends even with C if needed. Repeat on all C strips.

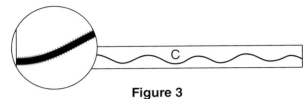

**Figure 3**

**7.** Trace the flower shape given on insert onto the fusible web as directed on the pattern; cut out, leaving a margin around each one. Fuse each flower shape onto the wrong side of the selected fat quarter. Cut out shapes on traced lines; remove paper backing.

**8.** Arrange and fuse one flower on each of five C strips and the remaining five flowers on one C strip referring to the Assembly Diagram for positioning suggestions.

**9.** Secure flower shapes in place using a narrow zigzag stitch.

**10.** Join the A-B rows with the C strips to complete the pieced top; press.

**11.** Create a quilt sandwich referring to Finishing Your Quilt on page 48.

**12.** Quilt as desired.

**13.** Bind referring to Finishing Your Quilt on page 48.

**14.** Fold the white print fat quarter in half with right sides together; pin to hold.

**Dream Weaver**
Assembly Diagram 66" x 78"

**15.** Trace 10 flower centers onto the wrong side of the pinned layers as shown in Figure 4; stitch on the marked lines as shown on flower center template.

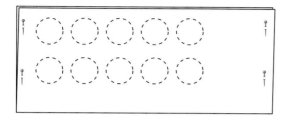

**Figure 4**

**16.** Cut out flower centers leaving at least ⅛" seam allowance all around as shown in Figure 5.

**Figure 5**

**17.** Cut a slit in one layer only of each flower center, being careful not to cut through the second layer; turn right side out through the slit. Press to make smooth edges.

**18.** Mark the star stitching line given on the pattern onto each pressed flower center using a water-erasable marker or pencil.

**19.** Using a doubled thread and a hand-stitching needle, stitch along the marked line; pull to gather and knot to make a gathered flower center referring to Figure 6; do not cut thread.

**Figure 6**

**20.** Center a button on the flower center; stitch in place; do not cut thread.

**21.** Center the flower center on a flower and hand-stitch in place to secure. ***Note:*** *If you don't want the stitches to show on the wrong side, be careful to keep stitches from going through the backing when stitching to the quilt top.*

**22.** Repeat steps 19–21 with each of the 10 flower centers to finish the quilt. ●

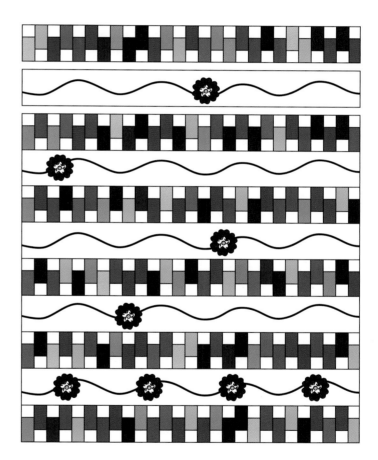

**Dream Weaver**
Alternate Assembly Diagram 54" x 66"
Use 27 A-B units in each row and eliminate 1 each pieced row and C strip to make this lap-size version.

# Wildflowers

A gentle mix of fusible wool appliqué and a traditional pieced batik background makes an extraordinary wall quilt that's perfect for any decor.

## Specifications

Skill Level: Intermediate
Quilt Size: 42¼" x 42¼"
Block Size: 9" x 9" finished
Number of Blocks: 12

## Materials

- Scraps red and green felted wool for leaves and berries
- Scraps assorted felted wool for flowers and stars
- ½ yard light gold batik
- ⅝ yard bright purple batik
- ¾ yard lavender/green batik
- 1⅔ yards white/oyster batik
- Backing to size
- Batting to size
- Thread
- 2 skeins green embroidery floss
- Embroidery floss to match felted wool
- 1½ yards 18"-wide lightweight fusible web
- Pencil or fine-point marker
- Basic sewing tools and supplies

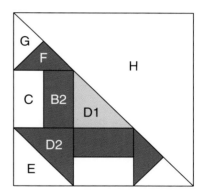

**Churn Dash**
9" x 9" Finished Block
Make 9

**Half Churn Dash**
9" x 9" Finished Block
Make 3

## Cutting

### From felted wool scraps:

- Cut leaves, berries, flowers and stars using templates given on insert as per instructions.

### From light gold batik:

- Cut 3 (2" by fabric width) B1 strips.
- Cut 2 (3⅞" by fabric width) strips.
  Subcut strips into 20 (3⅞") squares. Cut each square in half on 1 diagonal to make 40 D1 triangles; set aside 1 D1 triangle for your scrap basket.

### From bright purple batik:

- Cut 1 (4¼" by fabric width) strip.
  Subcut strip into 2 each 4¼" F and 3⅞" D2 squares. Cut the F squares on both diagonals to make 8 F triangles. Cut the D2 squares in half on 1 diagonal to make 4 D2 triangles; set aside 1 D2 and 2 F triangles for your scrap basket.
- Cut 1 (2" by fabric width) strip.
  Subcut strip into 6 (2" x 3½") B2 rectangles.
- Cut 5 (2¼" by fabric width) binding strips.

# Fusible Appliqué With Felted Wool

*Wash and dry wool, using no fabric softener, before preparing to use for appliqué.*

*Trace the appliqué shapes onto the paper side of the lightweight fusible web, leaving at least ¼" between shapes.*

*Cut out shapes leaving a margin around each one.*

*Fuse shapes to the wool using a pressing cloth or parchment paper between the iron and the shapes on the wool.*

*Cut out shapes on traced lines; remove paper backing.*

*Arrange the shapes with the fusible side down on the background fabric. When satisfied with placement, fuse pieces in place using parchment paper or a pressing cloth between the iron and the shapes.*

*Turn the fused area over and iron from the wrong side to complete the fusing process.*

*After fusing pieces in place, hand-stitch around edges of fused wool pieces using a blanket or buttonhole stitch with 3 strands of embroidery floss in colors to match each wool piece.*

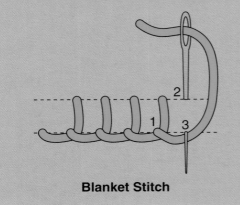

**Blanket Stitch**

## From lavender/green batik:

- Cut 1 (14" by fabric width) strip.
  Subcut strip into 1 each 14" J square, 9½" I square, one 9¼" O square and one 7¼" K square. Cut the J square on both diagonals to make 4 J triangles. Cut the K and O squares in half on 1 diagonal to make 2 each K and O triangles. Set aside 1 each J, K and O triangle for your scrap basket.
- Cut 3 (2½" by fabric width) strips.
  Trim 1 strip to make a 2½" x 40¾" P strip. Set aside remaining 2 strips for R.

## From white/oyster batik:

- Cut 1 (3½" by fabric width) strip.
  Subcut strip into 9 (3½") A squares.
- Cut 4 (2" by fabric width) C strips.
  Subcut 1 strip into 6 (2" x 3½") C rectangles.
- Cut 2 (3⅞" by fabric width) strips.
  Subcut strips into 20 (3⅞") squares. Cut each square in half on 1 diagonal to make 40 E triangles; set aside 1 triangle for your scrap basket.
- Cut 1 (14" by fabric width) strip.
  Subcut strip into 2 each 14" L squares and 4¼" G squares. Cut each L and G square on both diagonals to make 8 each L and G triangles; set aside 3 L and 2 G triangles for your scrap basket.
- Cut 1 (9⅞" by fabric width) strip.
  Subcut strip into 2 (9⅞") H squares and 1 (7¼") M square. Cut each square in half on 1 diagonal to make 4 H triangles and 2 M triangles; set aside 1 H triangle for your scrap basket.
- Cut 2 (2½" by fabric width) strips.
  Trim 1 strip to make a 2½" x 34" N strip and the second strip to make a 2½" x 40¾" Q strip.

## Completing the Churn Dash Blocks

**1.** Sew a B1 strip to a C strip with right sides together along length to make a B-C strip set; press. Repeat to make a total of three strip sets. Subcut strip sets into 36 (3½" x 3½") B-C units as shown in Figure 1.

B-C Unit
Cut 36

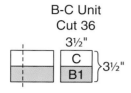

**Figure 1**

**2.** To complete one Churn Dash block, select one A square, and four each B-C units and D1 and E triangles.

**3.** Sew a D1 triangle to an E triangle to make a D-E unit as shown in Figure 2; press. Repeat to make a total of four D-E units.

D-E Unit
Make 4

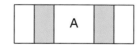

**Figure 2**          **Figure 3**

**4.** Sew a B-C unit to opposite sides of A to make the center row as shown in Figure 3; press.

**5.** Sew a D-E unit to opposite ends of each remaining B-C unit to make the top and bottom rows referring to Figure 4; press.

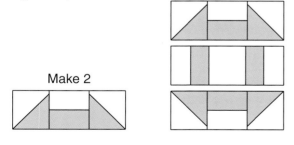

Make 2

**Figure 4**          **Figure 5**

**6.** Sew the center row between the top and bottom rows referring to Figure 5 to complete one Churn Dash block; press.

**7.** Repeat steps 2–6 to complete a total of nine Churn Dash blocks.

## Completing the Half Churn Dash Blocks

**1.** Select one each D1, D2, E and H triangle, and two each C and B2 rectangles and F and G triangles.

**2.** Sew B2 to C to make a B-C unit; repeat to make a second unit. Sew F to G to make one F-G unit and one reversed F-G unit, and D2 to E to make a D-E unit as shown in Figure 6; press.

B-C Unit
Make 2    F-G Unit    Reversed    D-E Unit
          Make 1    F-G Unit    Make 1
                    Make 1

**Figure 6**

**3.** Sew the F-G and reversed F-G units to the B-C units to make a side unit and reversed side unit as shown in Figure 7; press.

Side Units

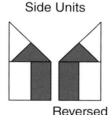

Reversed

**Figure 7**

**4.** Sew the D1 triangle to the B2 edge of the side unit and the D-E unit to one end of the reversed side unit as shown in Figure 8; press.

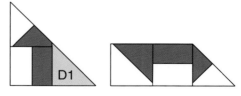

**Figure 8**

**5.** Join the units pieced in step 4 to make a triangle unit as shown in Figure 9; press.

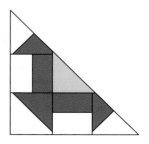

**Figure 9**

**6.** Sew the H triangle to the triangle unit to complete one Half Churn Dash block as shown in Figure 10; press.

**7.** Repeat steps 1–6 to complete a total of three Half Churn Dash blocks.

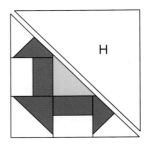

**Figure 10**

## Completing the Quilt

Refer to the Placement Diagram for positioning of pieces.

**1.** Arrange and join the pieced blocks in diagonal rows with the I square and the J, K, L and M triangles to complete the pieced center as shown in Figure 11.

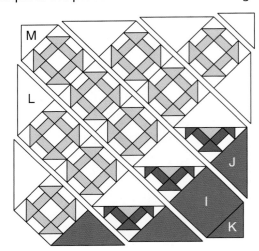

**Figure 11**

**2.** Sew the N strip to the left edge starting at the top edge and sewing to the bottom edge; press. Trim excess N strip even with the angled corner of the pieced center referring to Figure 12.

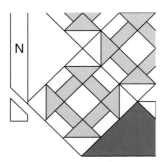

**Figure 12**

**3.** Sew the O triangle to the trimmed left bottom corner; press.

**4.** Sew the Q strip to the top and the P strip to the bottom of the pieced center; press seams toward strips.

**5.** Join the R strips on the short ends to make a long strip; press. Subcut strip into one 2½" x 42¾" strip. Sew the R strip to the right edge of pieced center to complete the quilt top; press.

**6.** Prepare flower pieces for appliqué referring to Fusible Appliqué With Felted Wool on page 22.

**7.** Arrange the flower, star, leaf and berry pieces on the quilt top and mark stem lines between them using a pencil or fine-point marker, adding some stems with curlicues using the photograph and pattern given as a guide.

**8.** Remove the flower, star, leaf and berry pieces. Using stem stitch and 3 strands of green embroidery floss, stitch along the marked stem lines.

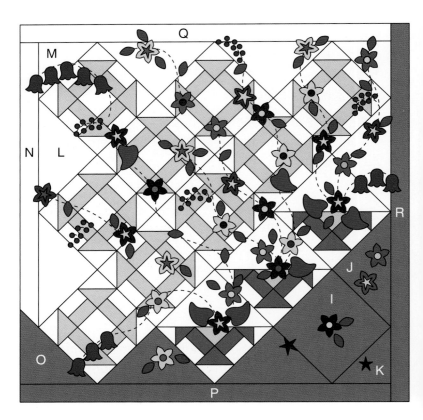

**Wildflowers**
Placement Diagram 42¼" x 42¼"

**9.** Place the flower, star, leaf and berry pieces at the ends of the stitched stem lines and around the remaining top as desired; fuse and stitch each shape in place referring to Fusible Appliqué With Felted Wool on page 22 to complete the appliqué.

**10.** Add French knots around the circular flower centers referring to Figure 13.

**Figure 13**

**11.** Create a quilt sandwich referring to Finishing Your Quilt on page 48.

**12.** Quilt as desired.

**13.** Bind referring to Finishing Your Quilt on page 48 to finish. ●

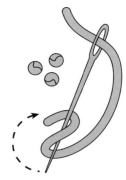

**French Knot**

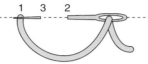

**Stem Stitch**

# Fulling or Felting Wool

Fulling or felting wool is the shrinking process used to make wool fabric or old woolen clothing into fabric that will not fray or stretch.

The process involves pouring boiling water over the wool, moving it around to make sure the fabric is completely soaked. Then rinse fabric and dry in a dryer on any setting. Dye will be released when the boiling water mixes with the wool fabric, so do not rinse different colors at the same time unless you want the dyes to migrate together.

Scraps of similar-color wools may be mixed together when rinsing with boiling water, but darker fabrics, especially red, should not be mixed with other colors when rinsing.

The thicker the original wool, the faster it will shrink. The thinner the original wool, the longer it will take to shrink.

If you have a large amount of wool to felt, place water in a large pot on your stove and heat water to boiling. You may place wool yardage in the pot, but remember not to mix colors together in the same water.

You may place the wool yardage in a washer and pour boiling water over it just enough to cover it and set the machine to agitate for about 10 minutes. At the end of this time, check the fabric to see if you can pull a thread from it; if you can, it will need more agitation. Continue until you can't pull any threads from the edge. Remove from the washer.

Remove the lint from the water with a strainer before allowing it to drain from the washer.

Return the wool to the washer and put through a cold-water rinse, removing any excess lint from the water again before allowing it to drain from the washer.

Place the rinsed wool in the dryer. Check the consistency of the felted wool after drying to be sure it is the thickness desired for appliqué.

Iron the wool with a spritzed pressing cloth.

# Fly Away Home

A collection of fabrics you love, some strip piecing and a bit of fusible appliqué are all you need to make this quilt happen. If this size isn't to your liking, there are plenty of size options.

## Specifications

Skill Level: Confident Beginner
Quilt Size: 87" x 96"
Block Sizes: 6⅜" x 6⅜" and 9" x 9" finished
Number of Blocks: 157 and 1

## Materials

- 1 fat quarter each 2 different burgundy prints
- Dark fabrics to total 4 yards
- Light fabrics to total 4½ yards
- 2⅛ yards brown multidot
- Backing to size
- Batting to size
- Thread
- 8" square ruler or larger
- Masking tape
- Template material
- 5 black seed beads
- Basic sewing tools and supplies

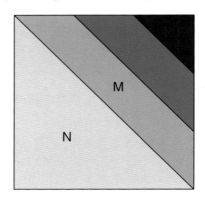

**Fly Away**
6⅜" x 6⅜" Finished Block
Make 157

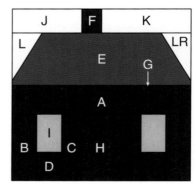

**House**
9" x 9" Finished Block
Make 1

## Cutting

Prepare pieces for appliqué using templates given on insert. Cut as per patterns and Needle-Turn Appliqué on page 32.

### From burgundy print 1:

- Cut 1 (1½" x 1¾") F rectangle.
- Cut 1 (1" x 9½") G strip.
- Cut 1 (2½" x 4") H rectangle.
- Cut bird body pieces as per pattern.

### From burgundy print 2:

- Cut bird upper and lower wing pieces as per pattern.

### From dark fabrics:

- Cut 61 (2" by fabric width) M strips.
- Select 1 fabric for house pieces.
    Cut 1 (2" x 9½") A rectangle.
    Cut 2 (1¾" x 4") B rectangles.
    Cut 2 (1½" x 4") C rectangles.
    Cut 2 (1¾" x 2") D rectangles.
- Select 1 fabric for roof.
    Cut 1 (3¼" x 9½") E rectangle.
- Select 1 fabric for windows.
    Cut 2 (1¾" x 2½") I rectangles.

## From light fabrics:

- Cut 81 (7¼") squares.
    Cut each square in half on 1 diagonal to make 162 N triangles; set aside 1 triangle for your scrap basket.
- Cut 8 (10¼") squares.
    Cut each square on both diagonals to make 32 O triangles. Set aside 3 triangles for your scrap basket.
- Select 1 fabric for House block background.
    Cut 1 (1¾" x 4") J rectangle.
    Cut 1 (1¾" x 5") K rectangle.
    Cut L and LR pieces as per pattern.

## From brown multidot:

- Cut 2 (2" by fabric width) M strips.
- Cut 9 (3½" by fabric width) P/Q strips.
- Cut 10 (2¼" by fabric width) binding strips.

## Completing the Fly Away Blocks

**1.** Select three M strips and join along the length, staggering 1½" at the ends to make an M strip set as shown in Figure 1; press. Repeat to make a total of 21 M strip sets.

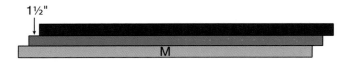

**Figure 1**

**2.** Place a piece of tape from the 7¼" mark on one side to the 7¼" mark on the adjacent side of the square ruler as shown in Figure 2.

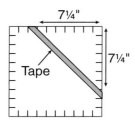

**Figure 2**

**3.** Place the marked ruler on one M strip set, aligning the top edge of the masking tape with the bottom edge of the strip, and cut one M triangle as shown in Figure 3.

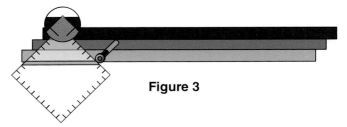

**Figure 3**

**4.** Continue cutting triangles across the strip, using both sides of the strip as shown in Figure 4. **Note:** *You should be able to cut eight triangles from each strip set.*

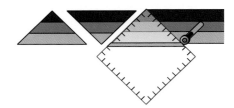

**Figure 4**

**5.** Repeat steps 3 and 4 to cut a total of 166 M triangles.

**6.** Sew an M triangle to an N triangle along the long diagonal edges to complete one Fly Away block as shown in Figure 5; press.

**Figure 5**

**7.** Repeat to make a total of 157 Fly Away blocks. Set aside remaining nine M triangles and four N triangles for setting the blocks together.

## Here's a Tip

*The edges of the strip-pieced sections of the blocks will be bias. Be careful not to stretch these edges when joining the blocks in diagonal rows.*

*Spray starch may be applied to these edges to help prevent stretching during handling.*

## Completing the House Block

**1.** Use the trimming template to trim one end of the E roof rectangle at an angle as shown in Figure 6. Reverse the template and trim the opposite end, again referring to Figure 6.

**Figure 6**

**2.** Sew L and LR pieces to E to complete the roof section as shown in Figure 7; press.

**Figure 7**

**3.** Sew F between J and K, and sew to the roof section to complete the sky/roof section as shown in Figure 8; press.

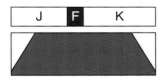

**Figure 8**

**4.** Sew I to D and add B and C to make a window unit as shown in Figure 9; press. Repeat to make a reversed window unit.

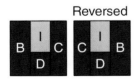

**Figure 9**

**5.** Referring to Figure 10, join the two window units with H; press. Add A to the long top edge to complete the house bottom section; press.

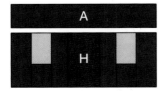

**Figure 10**

**6.** Fold the G strip in half along length with wrong sides together and align at the top of the A strip as shown in Figure 11; baste in place.

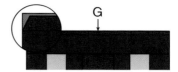

**Figure 11**

**7.** Join the house bottom and sky/roof section to complete the House block as shown in Figure 12.

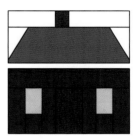

**Figure 12**

## Completing the Quilt

Refer to the Assembly Diagram for positioning of pieces.

**1.** Sew an N triangle to each side of the House block; press.

**2.** Arrange and join the Fly Away blocks in diagonal rows with the framed House block and the M and O triangles; press.

**3.** Join the rows to complete the quilt center; press.

## Here's a Tip

*I made four extra blocks to allow me to move blocks around to prevent fabric repeats in adjoining blocks. When the quilt top was finished, I joined the four remaining blocks as shown in Figure A. A bird motif was appliquéd to one of the light triangles. The block was pieced into the backing, signed and dated.*

**Figure A**

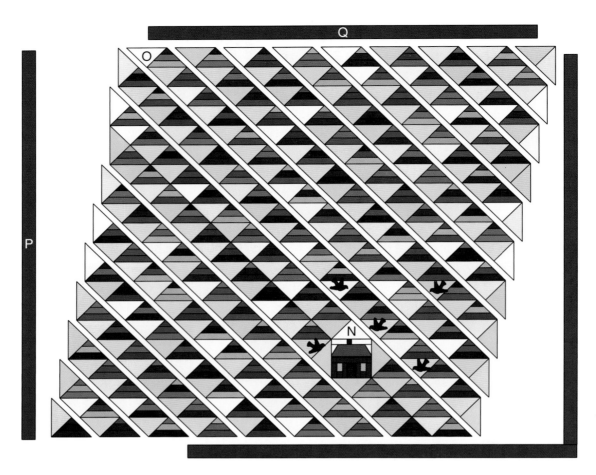

**Fly Away Home**
Assembly Diagram 87" x 96"

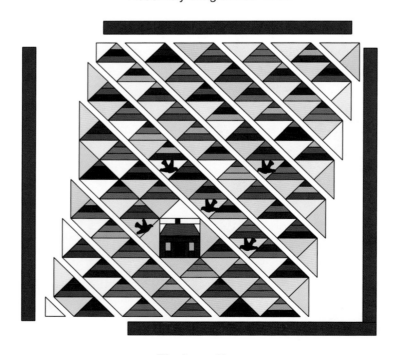

**Fly Away Home**
Alternate Assembly Diagram 55½" x 69"
Use 61 Fly Away blocks with 1 House block and cut
smaller-size triangles to fit on 2 corners to make a lap-size quilt.

**4.** Join the P/Q strips on the short ends to make a long strip; press. Subcut strip into two each 3½" x 90½" P strips and 3½" x 87½" Q strips.

**5.** Sew P strips to opposite long sides and Q strips to the top and bottom of the quilt center; press.

**6.** Prepare bird pieces for appliqué using patterns given and appliqué in place referring to Needle-Turn Appliqué on page 32.

**7.** Create a quilt sandwich referring to Finishing Your Quilt on page 48.

**8.** Quilt as desired.

**9.** Bind referring to Finishing Your Quilt on page 48 to finish.

**10.** Sew a seed bead to each bird for eyes to finish. ●

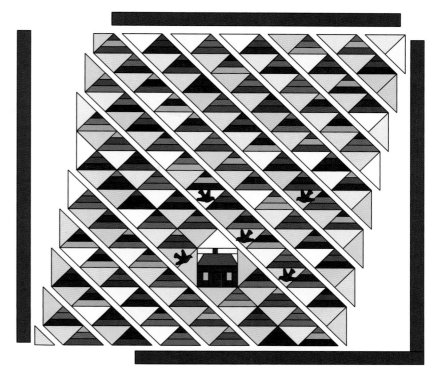

**Fly Away Home**
Alternate Assembly Diagram 64½" x 78"
Use 86 Fly Away blocks with 1 House block and cut smaller-size triangles to fit on 2 corners to make a twin-size quilt.

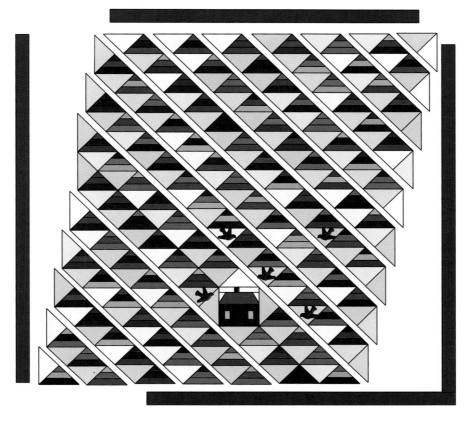

**Fly Away Home**
Alternate Assembly Diagram 69" x 87"
Use 106 Fly Away blocks with 1 House block to make a double-size quilt.

# Needle-Turn Appliqué

*Hand appliqué takes more time than fusible appliqué, but for some people the results are worth the extra time and effort. Here are two popular methods for hand appliqué. Refer to your favorite complete quilting guide for more methods.*

## Freezer-Paper Appliqué

**1.** Trace around the finished pattern size (do not include seam allowance on the pattern) on the paper side of a sheet of freezer paper. Reverse the pattern for any directional shapes before tracing (Figure A). Trace the number of pieces needed to complete the project.

**Figure A**

**2.** Cut out the freezer-paper shapes on the traced lines. You can layer, pin and cut three or four layers at a time without sacrificing accuracy.

**3.** Place and press the freezer-paper shapes with the waxy/shiny side down on the wrong side of the fabric leaving ½" between pieces (Figure B). The freezer-paper waxy/shiny side will stick to the fabric when heated and can be reused several times.

**Figure B**

**4.** Cut fabric pieces, leaving a ¼" seam allowance beyond the edge of the freezer-paper shape (Figure C).

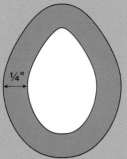

**Figure C**

**5.** Clip into curves almost to the paper shape (Figure D). Cut off sharp points ⅛"–¼" beyond the point of the freezer-paper pattern (Figure E). Clip into inside angles almost to the drawn line (Figure F).

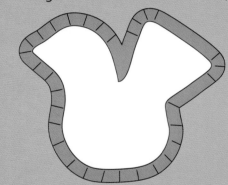

**Figure D**

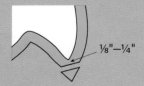

⅛"–¼"

**Figure E**

**Figure F**

**6.** Fold edges over the freezer paper and iron in place a little section at a time (Figure G). This is easier to accomplish if using a mini iron.

**Figure G**

**7.** When edges are smooth, remove freezer paper (Figure H).

**Figure H**

**8.** Position the prepared shape on the background. Blind-stitch piece in place using thread to match the fabric, insert a threaded needle into the folded edge and catch a few threads of the background before pulling out (Figure I). Stitches should not show.

**Figure I**

## Turned-Edge Appliqué

**1.** Prepare a template for the appliqué shape without seam allowance and trace around shape on the right side of the fabric using a fine-point pencil.

**2.** Cut out the shape ¼" beyond the marked line. Use thread to match the fabric to machine-stitch on the outside edge of the marked line (Figure J). Clip edges as shown in Figure D.

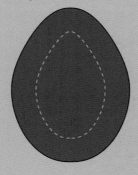

**Figure J**

**3.** Pin the cut shape in position on the background.

**4.** Turn in the fabric edge along the outer edge of the stitched line (Figure K). Blind-stitch the piece in place as you turn the edge in a little at a time (Figure L).

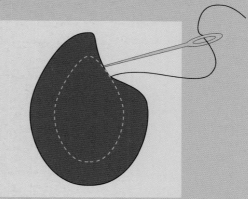

**Figure K**

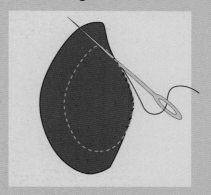

**Figure L**

## Tips

*Some quilters use a dab of fabric glue stick to hold the seam allowance in place on the freezer paper. This makes it a little more difficult to remove the freezer paper, but it does make the edges stick down and gives a crisp edge to the shape.*

*Mylar template plastic may be used instead of freezer paper. The pieces may be used over and over again.*

*Spray sizing (not spray starch) is another alternative that provides a stiff edge for turning.*

# Window to the Garden

Here's the perfect table set to accommodate your personal needs.
Make the runner and add the coordinating napkins for a unique look.

## Specifications

Skill Level: Intermediate
Runner Size: 48⅛" x 25½"
Napkin Size: 16" x 16"
Block Sizes: 14" x 14" and 6¼" x 6¼" finished
Number of Blocks: 2 each size

## Runner

### Materials

- 9 fat eighths coordinating fabrics
- ½ yard black solid
- ⅔ yards aqua solid
- Backing to size
- Batting to size
- Thread
- Basic sewing tools and supplies

## Cutting

### From fat eighths coordinating fabrics:

- Cut 1 (2½" x 21") strip each fabric.
  Subcut each strip into 8 (2½") A squares (72 total).
- Cut 2 of each of the following size pieces, cutting each size from a different fabric:
  2¼" E squares
  2¼" x 2¾" F rectangles
  2¼" x 4½" G rectangles
  2¼" x 5" H rectangles
  2¼" x 6¾" I rectangles.

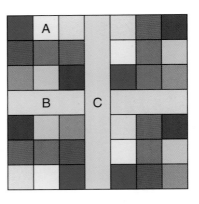

**Nine-Patch**
14" x 14" Finished Block
Make 2

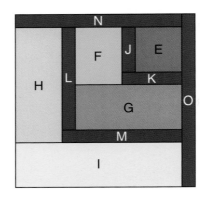

**Inside Corner Block**
6¼" x 6¼" Finished Block
Make 2

### From black solid:

- Cut 4 (2½" by fabric width) binding strips.
  Cut 1 (2½") Q square from the end of 1 strip.
- Cut 2 (1" by fabric width) strips.
  Subcut strips into 2 each of the following rectangles:

| | |
|---|---|
| 1" x 2¼" J | 1" x 5" M |
| 1" x 2¾" K | 1" x 6¾" N |
| 1" x 4½" L | 1" x 7¼" O |

## From aqua solid:

- Cut 1 (18½" by fabric width) strip.
  Subcut strip into the following:
  2 (2½" x 18½") P strips
  2 (2½" x 16½") D strips
  6 (2½" x 14½") C strips
  4 (2½" x 6½") B strips

## Completing the Nine-Patch Blocks

**1.** Select and join three A squares to make an A row as shown in Figure 1; press. Repeat to make a total of 24 A rows.

A Row
Make 24

**Figure 1**

**2.** Select three different A rows and join to make a block quarter as shown in Figure 2; press. Repeat to make a total of eight block quarters.

Block Quarter
Make 8

**Figure 2**

**3.** To complete one Nine-Patch block, select four block quarters, two B strips and one C strip.

**4.** Join two block quarters with a B strip to make a half-block as shown in Figure 3; press. Repeat.

Make 2

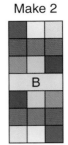

**Figure 3**

**5.** Join the two half-blocks with C to complete one Nine-Patch block referring to Figure 4; press.

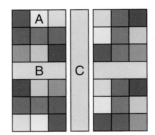

**Figure 4**

**6.** Repeat steps 3–5 to complete a second Nine-Patch block.

## Completing the Inside Corner Blocks

**1.** Select one each E square and F, G, H and I rectangle, and one each J, K, L, M, N and O strip to complete one Inside Corner block.

**2.** Sew J to E and add K as shown in Figure 5; press.

**Figure 5**

**3.** Add F to the J side and G to the K side of the pieced unit as shown in Figure 6; press.

   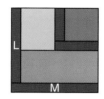

**Figure 6**        **Figure 7**

**4.** Add L to the F/G side and M to the G side of the pieced unit as shown in Figure 7; press.

**5.** Sew H to the L side and I to the M side of the pieced unit as shown in Figure 8; press.

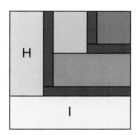

**Figure 8**

**6.** Add N to E/F/H side and O to the E/G/I side of the pieced unit to complete the block as shown in Figure 9; press.

**7.** Repeat steps 1–6 to complete a second Inside Corner block.

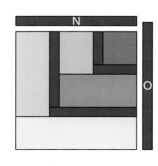

**Figure 9**

## Completing the Runner

Refer to the Assembly Diagram for positioning of blocks and strips.

**1.** Join the D strips with the Q square to make a D-Q strip; press.

**2.** Sew C strips to opposite sides and a P strip to one side of each Nine-Patch block; press.

**3.** Sew the Inside Corner blocks to the framed Nine-Patch blocks; press.

**4.** Join the pieced sections with the D-Q strip to complete the runner top; press.

**5.** Create a quilt sandwich referring to Finishing Your Quilt on page 48.

**6.** Quilt as desired.

**7.** Referring to Figure 10, trim batting and backing ¼" larger than the quilt top all around to make binding finish at ½" on the top side.

**Figure 10**

**8.** Bind referring to Finishing Your Quilt on page 48 to finish.

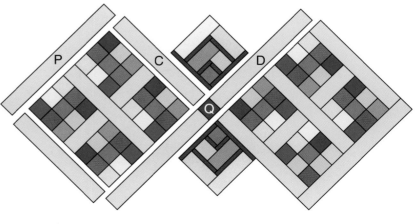

**Window to the Garden**
Assembly Diagram Approximately 48⅛" x 25½"

# Napkins

## Cutting

### From aqua solid:

- Cut 2 (17" by fabric width) strips. Subcut strips into 4 (17") squares.

## Completing the Napkins

**1.** Turn under the edge of one aqua solid square ¼" and press. Turn under ¼" again, press and stitch to hem the napkin as shown in Figure 11. Repeat with all aqua solid squares.

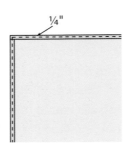

**Figure 11**

**2.** Cut eight 1¾" squares and four 2" squares fusible web. Fuse the 1¾" squares to the wrong side of the coordinating fabric squares and the 2" squares to the wrong side of the black tonal squares. Cut along the edges of the fusible web squares.

**3.** Cut a 1¼" square out of the center of each fused black square to make a frame piece as shown in Figure 12.

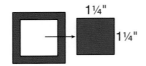

**Figure 12**

**4.** Remove paper backing from all squares and the frame pieces. Arrange and fuse two 1¾" coordinating fabric squares on one corner of one napkin referring to Figure 13 for positioning.

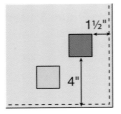
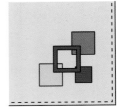

**Figure 13**      **Figure 14**

**5.** Center and fuse a black frame between the two fused squares, tucking a 1¼" black square under the bottom right-hand corner of the frame before fusing in place referring to Figure 14.

**6.** Using black thread on the black pieces and thread to match fabrics on the other squares, machine zigzag-stitch around edges to secure and finish the napkin.

**7.** Repeat steps 4–6 on the remaining hemmed napkins to complete the set of four. ●

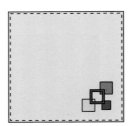

**Window to the Garden Napkin**
Placement Diagram 16" x 16"

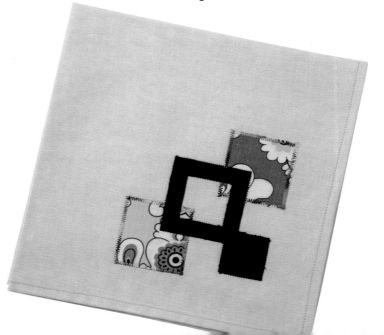

# Here's a Tip

*To reduce bulk when binding the inside corners of the runner, you may want to use a single-fold bias binding. The bias binding will stretch to accommodate the stretch on the inside corner, and the single layer will help decrease the bulk of the seams in those corners where the blocks join.*

**1.** To make single-fold bias binding, cut 1¾"-wide bias strips from the black solid. Join the strips on the short ends to make a 150"-long strip.

**2.** Fold ¼" to the wrong side on one long edge and press to hold.

**3.** Staystitch close to the ¼" seam allowance through the layers of the runner at each inside corner as shown in Figure A.

**Figure A**

**4.** Clip into the corner almost to the seam allowance as shown in Figure B.

**Figure B**

**5.** Leaving a 12" tail, match the raw edge of the binding to the raw edge of the runner top and stitch using a ¼" seam allowance, mitering at the outer corners.

**6.** Sew the binding to the edge of each inside corner, leaving the needle down at the clip as shown in Figure C.

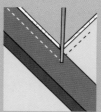

**Figure C**

**7.** Turn the runner top and sew along the adjacent side of the inside corner.

**8.** Continue sewing binding all around, overlapping at the beginning and end.

**9.** Clip into each inside corner of binding just to the stitching line referring to Figure D.

**Figure D**

**10.** To sew the binding down at the inside corners, referring to Figure E, fold down the left side and then the right side and hand-stitch the miter that forms. Turn to the back side and repeat to complete the binding.

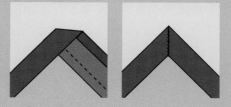

**Figure E**

This method also works with a double-layered binding.

# Autumn Leaves

## A classic favorite in autumn's warm palette will surely make any room cozy.

## Specifications
Skill Level: Confident Beginner
Quilt Size: 64" x 64"
Block Size: 6" x 6" finished
Number of Blocks: 20

## Materials
- 20 leaf-color batik scraps at least 8" square
- ½ yard light gold batik
- ⅝ yard cream batik
- ⅝ yard black solid
- 1⅛ yards orange/green batik
- 2⅛ yards brown/orange batik
- Backing to size
- Batting to size
- Thread
- Basic sewing tools and supplies

## Cutting

### From leaf-color batik scraps:
- Cut the following from each scrap:
    3 (2½") A squares
    2 (2⅞") B squares
    1 (1" x 3½") E stem strip

### From light gold batik:
- Cut 4 (3½" by fabric width) strips.
    Trim to 3½" x 36½" I strips.

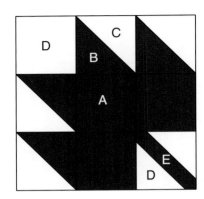

**Maple Leaf**
6" x 6" Finished Block
Make 20

### From cream batik:
- Cut 3 (2⅞" by fabric width) strips.
    Subcut strips into 40 (2⅞") C squares.
- Cut 3 (2½" by fabric width) strips.
    Subcut strips into 40 (2½") D squares.

### From black solid:
- Cut 7 (2¼" by fabric width) binding strips.

### From orange/green batik:
- Cut 5 (6⅞" by fabric width) strips.
    Subcut strips into 28 (6⅞") F squares.

### From brown/orange batik:
- Cut 5 (6⅞" by fabric width) strips.
    Subcut strips into 28 (6⅞") G squares.
- Cut 4 (3½" by fabric width) strips.
    Trim to 3½" x 36½" H strips.
- Cut 6 (2½" by fabric width) J/K strips.

## Completing the Maple Leaf Blocks

**1.** Mark a diagonal line from corner to corner on all C squares.

**2.** Select one set of same-fabric A, B and E pieces, and two each C and D squares.

**3.** Referring to Figure 1, place a C square right sides together with a B square; stitch ¼" on each side of the marked line. Cut apart on the marked line and press units open to make two B-C units. Repeat to make a total of four B-C units.

**Figure 1**

**4.** Cut one D square in half on one diagonal. Referring to Figure 2, center and sew the E stem strip between the two D triangles; press. Trim to 2½" with E centered to complete a D-E unit.

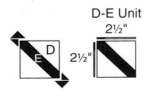

**Figure 2**

**5.** Arrange and join the B-C units with the A and D squares and the D-E unit to make three rows as shown in Figure 3; press. Join the rows to complete one Maple Leaf block; press.

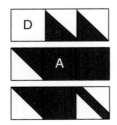

**Figure 3**

**6.** Repeat steps 2–5 to complete a total of 20 Maple Leaf blocks.

## Completing the Quilt

Refer to the Assembly Diagram for positioning of pieces.

**1.** Mark a diagonal line from corner to corner on the wrong side of each F square.

**2.** Referring to Figure 4, place an F square right sides together with a G square and stitch ¼" on each side of the marked line. Cut apart on the marked line and press open to complete one F-G unit. Repeat to make a total of 56 F-G units.

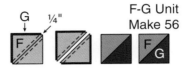

**Figure 4**

**3.** Join two F-G units to make a side unit as shown in Figure 5; press. Repeat to make a total of 28 side units.

**Figure 5**

**4.** Arrange and join 12 Maple Leaf blocks with 12 side units to make the center unit as shown in Figure 6; press.

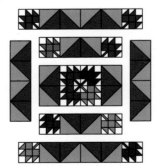

**Figure 6**

**5.** Sew an H strip to an I strip along length to make an H-I strip set; press. Repeat to make a total of four H-I strip sets.

**6.** Sew an H-I strip set to opposite sides of the center unit with H strips toward the center; press. Sew a Maple Leaf block to the end of each remaining H-I strip set; press. Sew these strips to the top and bottom of the center unit; press.

**7.** Join four side units to make a side strip; press. Repeat to make a total of four side strips.

**8.** Sew a side strip to opposite sides of the bordered center unit; press.

**9.** Sew a Maple Leaf block to each end of each remaining side strip; press. Sew these strips to the top and bottom of the bordered center unit to complete the quilt top; press.

**10.** Join the J/K strips on the short ends to make a long strip; press. Subcut strip into two each 2½" x 60½" J strips and 2½" x 64½" K strips.

**11.** Sew J strips to opposite long sides and K strips to the top and bottom of the quilt center; press.

**12.** Create a quilt sandwich referring to Finishing Your Quilt on page 48.

**13.** Quilt as desired.

**14.** Bind referring to Finishing Your Quilt on page 48 to finish. ●

## Here's a Tip

*If you are using a stripe fabric for the G triangles, cut the pieces to create a perpendicular corner where the F-G units meet as shown in Figure A. To do this, you will need to have the straight-of-grain edge on the long diagonal sides and bias edges on the short sides of the G triangles in the F-G units. Cut 4⅞" by fabric-width strips and cut triangles with 6⅞" short sides and a 9¾" long edge as shown in Figure B.*

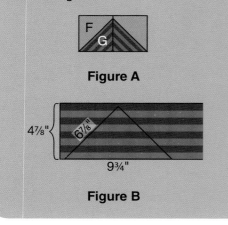

**Figure A**

**Figure B**

**Autumn Leaves**
Assembly Diagram 64" x 64"

# Double Arrow

Basic traditional piecing and your favorite fabrics
are all you need to create this masterpiece.

## Specifications

Skill Level: Confident Beginner
Quilt Size: 67" x 81¼"
Block Size: 10" x 10" finished
Number of Blocks: 32

## Materials

- 32 (4½") A squares assorted medium fabrics
- ⅝ yard medium gray tonal
- ⅔ yard dark gray solid
- 2½ yards total dark fabrics
- 4½ yards total light background fabrics
- Backing to size
- Batting to size
- Thread
- Basic sewing tools and supplies

## Cutting

### From medium gray tonal:

- Cut 7 (2½" by fabric width) J/K strips.

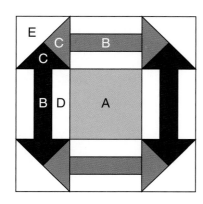

**Double Arrow**
10" x 10" Finished Block
Make 32

### From dark gray solid:

- Cut 8 (2¼" by fabric width) binding strips.

### From dark fabrics:

- Cut 64 matching sets of 2 (1½" x 4½") B rectangles and 1 (4¼") C square (128 B rectangles and 64 C squares total).

### From light background fabrics:

- Cut 32 matching sets of 2 (3⅞") E squares and 8 (1½" x 4½") D rectangles (64 E squares and 256 D rectangles total).
- Cut 4 (15½") squares.
    Cut each square on both diagonals to make 16 F triangles; set aside 2 F triangles for your scrap basket.
- Cut 2 (8") squares.
    Cut each square in half on 1 diagonal to make 4 G triangles.
- Cut 3½"-wide rectangles in a variety of lengths to equal a total of 275" when joined for H/I strips.

## Completing the Blocks

**1.** To complete one Double Arrow block, select one A square, two different sets of two B rectangles each and one C square (four B rectangles and two C squares total), and one set of two E squares and eight D rectangles.

**2.** Sew a B rectangle between two D rectangles to make a B-D unit as shown in Figure 1. Repeat to make a second matching B-D unit to make a set. Repeat to make a second set.

Make 2 each

**Figure 1**

**3.** Draw a diagonal line from corner to corner on one C and both E squares.

**4.** Place the marked C square right sides together with the unmarked C square and stitch ¼" on each side of the marked line. Cut apart on the marked line to make two C units as shown in Figure 2; press.

**Figure 2**

**Figure 3**

**5.** Place the marked E square right sides together on one C unit with the marked line crossing the C seam line and stitch ¼" on each side of the marked line as shown in Figure 3.

**6.** Cut apart on the marked line to make one each C-E and reversed C-E unit as shown in Figure 4; press.

C-E Units
Make 2 each

Reversed

**Figure 4**

**7.** Repeat steps 5 and 6 with the remaining C unit and E square to make a total of two each C-E and reversed C-E units.

**8.** Sew a C-E and reversed C-E unit to opposite ends of two matching B-D units, matching the B and C fabrics to make a row as shown in Figure 5; press. Repeat to make a second row.

Make 2

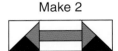

**Figure 5**

**9.** Sew the remaining matching B-D units to opposite sides of A to make the center row as shown in Figure 6; press.

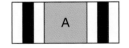

**Figure 6**

**10.** Join the rows as shown in Figure 7 to complete one Double Arrow block; press.

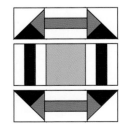

**Figure 7**

**11.** Repeat all steps to complete a total of 32 Double Arrow blocks.

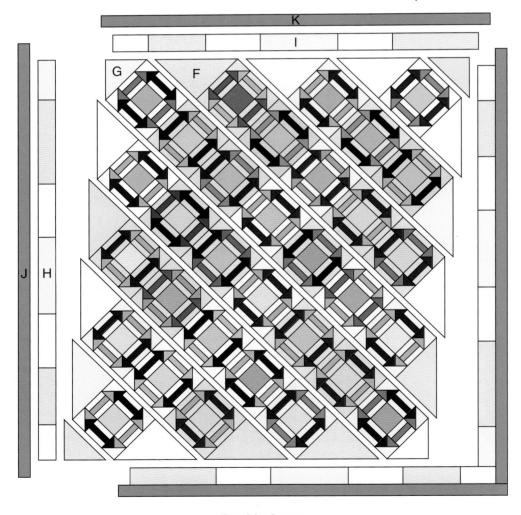

**Double Arrow**
Assembly Diagram 67" x 81¼"

## Completing the Quilt

Refer to the Assembly Diagram for positioning of pieces.

**1.** Arrange and join the Double Arrow blocks in diagonal rows with the F and G triangles; press.

**2.** Join the rows to complete the quilt center; press.

**3.** Join the H/I rectangles on the short ends to make a 275"-long strip; press. Subcut strip into two each 3½" x 71¾" H strips and 3½" x 63½" I strips.

**4.** Sew the H strips to opposite long sides and I strips to the top and bottom of the quilt center; press.

**5.** Join the J/K strips on the short ends to make a long strip; press. Subcut strip into two each 2½" x 77¾" J strips and 2½" x 67½" K strips.

**6.** Sew the J strips to opposite long sides and K strips to the top and bottom of the quilt center to complete the quilt top; press.

**7.** Create a quilt sandwich referring to Finishing Your Quilt on page 48.

**8.** Quilt as desired.

**9.** Bind referring to Finishing Your Quilt on page 48 to finish. ●

## Here's a Tip

*Pin the pieces together in sets after cutting to make it easier later when selecting the matching sets to make the blocks.*

**Double Arrow**
Alternate Assembly Diagram 52¾" x 67"
Eliminate 2 long diagonal rows
to make a lap-size version of this quilt.

# Finishing Your Quilt

**1.** Press quilt top on both sides; check for proper seam pressing and trim all loose threads.

**2.** Sandwich batting between the stitched top and the prepared backing piece; pin or baste layers together to hold. Mark quilting design and quilt as desired by hand or machine.

**3.** When quilting is complete, remove pins or basting. Trim batting and backing fabric edges even with raw edges of quilt top.

**4.** Join binding strips on short ends with diagonal seams to make one long strip; trim seams to ¼" and press seams open.

**5.** Fold the binding strip in half with wrong sides together along length; press.

**6.** Sew binding to quilt edges, matching raw edges, mitering corners and overlapping ends.

**7.** Fold binding to the back side and stitch in place to finish.

# Special Thanks

We would like to thank the following manufacturers and quilters who provided materials and quilting services to make sample projects for this book.

**Autumn Leaves, page 40:** Hoffman California fabrics; Nature-Fil™ bamboo-blend batting from Fairfield.

**Black Tie Event, page 8:** Timeless Treasures fabrics; Fusi-Boo® fusible blended-fiber batting from Fairfield.

**Double Arrow, page 45:** European Taupe by Kinkame for Clothworks; Nature-Fil™ bamboo-blend batting from Fairfield.

**Dream Weaver, page 16:** Rowan Classics by Kaffe Fassett for Westminster Fabrics; Nature-Fil™ bamboo-blend batting from Fairfield; quilted by Lynette Gelling.

**Fly Away Home, page 26:** European Taupe by Kinkame for Clothworks; Nature-Fil™ bamboo-blend batting from Fairfield; quilted by Cindy Messervey.

**Friends, page 3:** Batik fabrics from Hoffman of California; Fusi-Boo® fusible blended-fiber batting from Fairfield.

**Lily & Friends, page 11:** Fabrics from Hoffman of California; Fusi-Boo® fusible blended-fiber batting and Poly-Fil® fiberfill from Fairfield.

**Wildflowers, page 21:** Hoffman California fabrics; American Spirit 70/30 batting from Fairfield.

**Window to the Garden, page 34:** Amy Butler fabrics from Westminster Fabrics; Fusi-Boo® fusible fleece from Fairfield.